LION'S PAW

KATHLEEN PEIRCE

Lion's Paw

MIAMI UNIVERSITY PRESS

Library of Congress Cataloging-in-Publication Data
Names: Peirce, Kathleen, 1956– author.
Title: Lion's paw / Kathleen Peirce.
Description: Oxford : Miami University Press, [2021]
Identifiers: LCCN 2020032375 | ISBN 9781881163688 (trade paperback)
Subjects: LCGFT: Poetry.
Classification: LCC PS3566.E34 L56 2021 | DDC 811/.54—dc23
LC record available at https://lccn.loc.gov/2020032375

Designed by Crisis
Cover painting: Ilya Zomb,
Sphinx Guarding the Sleep of Mnemosyne.
Oil on canvas, copyright © 1995.
Printed on acid-free, recycled paper
in the United States of America

Miami University Press
356 Bachelor Hall
Miami University
Oxford, Ohio 45056

Many thanks to publications where
some of these poems have appeared:
Blue River, Crazyhorse, Cutbank,
Diagram, February, Fifth Wednesday Journal,
Gulf Coast Review, Ilanot Review, Ploughshares,
The Laurel Review, The Literati Quarterly,
Tupelo Quarterly, White Whale Review.
For The Whiting Foundation, and the John
Simon Guggenheim Foundation, many thanks.

LION'S PAW

That's right,
left where a trace
crosses between persons
and things. Some say
dances not crosses. Not this time.

BIRTHDAY EVE

Is it luscious there? Nightless, dayless,
one made as a parallelogram is made, with no part
not itself? Regardless, a visitor in visitor's quarters
must come to the door, and soon. First,
flex against an amnion ripe with angels
singing with their breasts exposed, impossible to know
as what red is, though all will be glazed
and caught by reddening tomorrow, uncountable
angels with their breasts revealed, milk-heavy,
all resting on all sides,
the singing to return again inside the voices
heard submerged inside a lake in time, as one comes
to understand a peacock's feeling, opening out its tail
of faces started in an infant's eggs, O animal's animal,
O fruit-foot, O oblong, crown-down form
so roped to form for good.

A FEATHER

All the birds that ever were
are with this tail part that seems dreaming
alone and in a human hand,
its stripes tiger stripes, banded like that, but
black and rosy brown, unmoving while waving
from the center, out and up like an intention or
momentum toward an end we will be finished being with,
to look back at from an afterward, if not
an afterlife, or if from an afterlife, maybe to have
relief from a relentless sense of moving toward.
As of yet, we're still where a feather leaves a tiger
at a wider band of black, signaling, maybe, the end of empathy
or it may be the only answer to the iridescent band
that's coming next, as it must, made for clanging toward
and away from light, giddy turkey tail, someone testing the extent
of vertigo, faithfulness angling toward despair,
despair lessened by a feast. Some never think
there could be other, better languages, even when delivered
to the pale, free edge, the paleness arrayed there, on its terms.

ROSES ARE PLANTED WHERE THORNS GROW

Especially at dusk, why not
feel touched, stepped away from thought
by the quiet of a photograph of a forest at nightfall
taken down from the tension of its nail,
touch touching what it wants
but from a distant place. One feels
a whole forest can be held, is quiet, too,
when entered first by someone else's eye. One is forested
as who would fix an ear to a seashell named Lion's Paw
to hear a lion roar. This seems what dusk can ask of us.

Day asks another way. Thought like a needle, an atlatl
of one's own will or helplessness, singular,
sharp, though soft at the start, supple as a bone in infancy,
alloyed there, to wet the thread for, pierce the eye of,
load the cup, make leverage, extend the loaded human arm:
amentum, woomera, *the eye is lion of these wastes*
whose visions tear the carcase loose
or it binds an edge, or for pleasure might
embroider something there.
Dusk like a touch. Thought like a needle.
Dream like a flower well beyond a town where people say
In my house are shapes of flowers I have never seen.

TABLEAU

Life pursues me like a shadow. —Fernando Pessoa

Dry odor of dust. The yellow room a box
inside the light, the light so hot and mean. Long
June. What moved inside had voices, or made sounds
to think of as voices. One oak branch tip
was brought to touch the house by wind. *We would*
come in. The only pendulum, repaired, returned
the day before, was set too near its chimes, and made
a metallic slogan as it swung, changed from what had been
remembered as a happy, wooden pulse.
It pinched the air. *Pit take Pit take*. What does
a resident of earth deserve? Not to hear entirety,
like a planet seen, or as a faded part, a closed room with no stairs.
A person wants to want to move across a room, capable at heart
to make no sound and pull the curtain back, or down.

SOFT GROUND

I saw a grave. One rolag rolled down from a thigh onto the floor
and could only be reached by being lifted
up by toes. Every spinster knows a spinning wheel turns but cannot roll
away. Some shapes bring hands to hold.

A rolag is a coil of fibers blended on a blending board
before they will be spun. That rolag held light fawn alpaca,
golden merino wool, a tan merino, a soft orange,
and silk dyed as lilacs pulled from under muddy water,

with a gloss of water. If you spend your life making smaller things,
your back will roll forward when you stand. Have you seen the filament
a silk cocoon lets go, its singularity upheld *and* unwound, unspooled
as tongues above the vats as mothers singing lullabies in heaven,

all the same and still particular? Have you seen the silk cocoon
a sister to an egg? In a playhouse, two red shoes can be left facing the door
as though a girl transcended, and remains. An alpaca seems happy
when its softness is shorn, though it is held down, and eyes

see eyes roll back in fear when one is pinned. All yarn must twist. One cure
for back pain is to wait, in bed, on ice. Silvery branches of a shrub, a young rain sage,
are supple and will toss, buoyant like a girl you remember though a long time passed,
and though so thirsty in dry ground. Seen from your bed, you can wave back or not.

MORE

Some things are prettier than the day, and some
will force lightheadedness onto thinking about them. Small
animals, named with fairness and precaution, bring us
their movements from sleep to sleep, as though
in conversation with our conversation.

People can have trouble with fire, begging, endlessness, as
night begins, but most erase the heaviness from an evening sun
right after it sinks. Without needing to think, a dog prepares a bed
by circling. When from the wet point on a spiral,
dreams approach, most nights increase themselves
like wings, like a tumbler of perfume in flames. To wear?
To speak about? To beg us always toward release?

THIS WAY

No pre-
face;

a pre-way
(pre-via)
(pre-vious)

heard-at-
heart

voice is
heard
to say,

Speak.
Speech makes

faces.

PLAY OF CAUSES

Two trees there beyond the shore
mark where the pale lake has made
a perfect distant zig-zag in the view
from the clay window with two arches
and one post. The viewer disregards the view,
looks neither at the window nor through, but forward
across the table where the right hand draws
a face in profile, whose?, and the left
is a weight on the sheet.

IN SUMMER

Another mud dauber, more wasp-waisted
than a girl, has come in, on
spring's call, to window-walk
like things wake, up. In each *begun again*
the getting-out is blunt, denied,

like pain wakes, inside,
its presence wholly understood where, before,
its absence had been only partly realized: no rancor, no slander,
about as luscious as boniness held against a wall
of glass. Holy Spirit, come. Bring getting/giving over.

BOUND TO LOWER

Crescent moon. Knife
over meat. One hand raised like that,
sure, but the
other hand—which things are its things?
Lion in Eden,
crouched between him and her,
why didn't you, why didn't you
before the word fell out
spring up
flower

TWO HORSES IN A FIELD WITH DAFFODILS

are eating daffodils. Near the word daffodil,
yellow is uncalled-for and still found, because the two

are beautiful together. Yellow daffodil, daffodil
yellow. By the same means, the sky is always blue

when said so by two people across a world-wide gap,
and said only to each other. Do you see in your head

two daffodils in a water glass, helpless
not to face different directions? Still

they are the same. The farmers of Latium used to say,
with the Tiber (*flavus*, the blond) flooding through

the same yellows as now, that the fields were thirsty
and the vines going mad. When I understand

I extend my mind like horse lips to a flower
and take in the thing. When I don't understand,

I make things out of myself and become them,
transforming myself into them. Horse lips wet on canary

yellow flown and held in mind.

CUL-DE-SAC

It was a personal watermelon
that rolled in its bag
down the driveway
to the road
eaten to a thin, bagged
dew pond of juice
by morning's raised wing
it was a strange wren
that got in the house, though
it was a house wren
on the cul-de-sac
where no neighbors speak.

WHITE WITH OFF-WHITE

Of today's alligator cloud or
this little plush toy dog, which is more
soaked through with future falling,
which silkworm collapsed into the fluffiest wings
inside its self-made tellurian cocoon,
having nothing to do with anyone
but holding auspices like fingers are
almost thoughtful on the neck of a guitar,
the song about to start, the song about
to be composed, as true in accrual
as dissolve, from where the preparations have begun
beside the dead, each of us in expectation of ascending notes
from way over here and listening.

ANIMA FORMA CORPORIS

—Aquinas

In a November of false weather, overwarm,
green shoots showed
and she could not see them,
wrapped as she was,
indoors, in a cranberry sweater, tan slacks,
eighty-eight years, though these fall loose
in recognition now, and away
in increments even the closest view would
not catch, not make clear.
As with the out-movement of a leaf
one would like to have seen happening, one would;
too late. The body has arrived.

BLUISH

There's a knife
in the word *precision.* I would cut
it out. I would cut across it as a squall line
coming to the limit of how long a dry sky can be listened to,
falling in with suddenness itself
while also happening in increments as all things are,
at once close by and far away like sleep, like a sad dream getting ready
the next day's tears, the creek about to be so opulent,
verbose after that thunderstorm
after that year of dust.
Let's see how you're made is what a lover says. Let's see. And then
the drought comes back, expected now.
Look how it begins, at what was once creekside, touching the one vine
of bluish flower-cups still spiraling up its branch of ordinary undergrowth,
blurring life for them, as when I sensed a rain and stepped outside to cut
my body into it to find a hard rain falling from a sky still blue, regardless,
irregardless, nonetheless, and all the more.

OUTLINE FOR FLIGHT

A sinker does one thing.
I've been dense, a vegetable, voile between layers
of itself. I've honored one virtue like the substance in a cell,
or shell, or crinoline, whirled there, whorled,
environmental. A nest is a mine
where siblings tunnel through the part
of earth called hen. Feelings in the soil
express themselves as tourmaline
or not, but tourmaline occurs. Inside,
outside, one wing will always mean immobility.

WE WERE IN A BIG CAFÉ IN PARIS

A note could arrive today from someone traveling,
someone unseen descending six staircases
for black radishes in Paris, someone made visible
by sentences alone, each set a flight
as are the colors of the passersby
moving across and then beyond a city window,
seen maybe from inside a big café, colors prepared to go
somewhere, petals as we have agreed, or
last night's sunset passed across a canyon
under what a Texan calls the largest sky, best flower colors overhead,
good water movements in the air's striations, a bleeding through
following so beautifully the final flash,
as of a lid closing on a velvet box and its opal quivering.

MOBILE

See how
having climbed
a trellis of white roses
hangs beside saying so, as when
at another end of a curved wire
a weight in kind is added, and the
gestures can begin.

OVATION

Do you remember hearing the end, and past the end
of one leaf's fall? Can we still be children there?
The subject still is love. The leaf would fall. I offer
this photograph: a vision of a fallen leaf with ovate shape,
though I'd prefer to lay across this line the low notes of an oboe
were it obovate. It was ovate, on its back, verso, salver
for two round shapes I've taken as a child to be spider eggs
and so still do. Some may have been—
an inundation, sealed—
Has the oboe gone completely quiet now? I took a note
while standing at a pencil drawing of a pair:
of course one sees / the faces first /
one leans to touch / forehead to the other's cheek /
only after this / the eye goes down / to the already
joined hands

Returning to the moment of the leaf: it always was too late
to say *don't fall.* Our subject still is love. The leaf's ending
had occurred because beginning had begun, some forms held on,
and someone's eye has added grandeur there,
grandeur of finish we know as host to the sublime
which now involves these orbs, one left one right
of the primary vein. It holds them, or they hold onto it,
or both. I would like to fold this leaf in half with thoughts,
to put them side by side. If not
two eggs, is this a view of the relationship between

leaf and fruiting body? Both species benefit, if so—
Another drawing: odalisque. Another note:
round face / round hair /
round breasts / round hand / herself
at hand

Are you with me? Do we end
more helpless quieted
or increased? We are come toward.
We started as children here.
How many leaves were in the photograph? Right. Yes.
All the leaves that ever were.

THIS WAY

No pre-
face;

face that

passes faces

sees sometimes

is passed
sometimes

sometimes sees

the way

a clementine's
segments touch—

skin-dressed,
delicious,

like,
unlike.

I DON'T KNOW HOW TO MAKE A MAN

On paper, in my hand, with my eyes, I find
my great grandfather on the side edge
of a hardwood chair, up on a hip
with his legs crossed, with his hat
pushed back, with his forehead torn by a fleck like a shot
had rung, but he smiles.
My own face as a child comes to mind
like light displaced on lake water by an oar
in my father's hand. And
I had read the sentence *here we have a stone earlobe*
absorbing the prayers of an ancient Egyptian
the day the couple came to fix the clock,
a grandfather, taller than. They moved, at work,
like fewer than two animals, more than one flower, his gentle
removal of the face, her hand holding the door away,
their one voice low, asking for tools across which
tools were passed, with the heartbeat stopped, her white gloves on,
his shoulder back inside, his hand so lightly
hitting the notes out of sequence wildly, with my son still
not come home for years. Absorb, lobe of stone,
because we are first sensual, and then must be rich.

TOKENS

from inside, a light rain without sound so
the loquat appears to weep

*

inner compartment of the prayer wheel
bearing the no-weight of one name

*

stems continue, but with
orchid buds now

*

photograph of a room sent
in place of the photographer returning

*

distressing every feeding bird
one mockingbird

*

of self-portraits, the sensation
in touching paint to one's mouth

*

the relation of the hands to the face
after good dreams, after nightmares

*

rain harder now, a return
awareness of the usual way things fall

FIRST THE FAWN

First the fawn dropped,
born, then walked away,
lowered and folded itself back
down when the dog came running
also with legs
from mottled grasses
sprang the year's first cicada
vibrating itself refusing to leave
now on the window through which
less and less is clear.

CORRIDOR

A little flood water rising to the teeth,
a little wave wringing out the nest
I speak of, speak from. I am
wrung from what were wings once
and still are. Behind us now,
the bowerbird's walkway lined with shards
of violets, eyes of feathers, fireberries hung on thorns,
all the bowing done, your look swinging down
the closer your face comes, this time
after your death, and from now on.

AT INTERVALS

At intervals, new birds arrive. Seeing will seem a gesture
offered back to them, a swinging up to meet their swinging down,
fate made simple by surprise but requiring a changeless act,
as one steps into one's chamber on a ferris wheel
differently than any other place, as flying first means flying up,
or sitting, sitting down. Before I was moved, I could hear feathers
affect feathers overhead. Sensation of being swung
backward, off, into a fate only a practiced bird would think
to sing, not a feather, not a wing, the whole body
averted, then arrived, and with such a view, as with pain or love.

THIS WAY

No pre-
face;

blankpage. An
egg's face is

where?

O,

but inside

but inside

suspended—

crack it out

ELEGY IN WINTER

Goes missing,
lilac. Goes,
peony. Inundated
sunflower,
my only mother,
our stem-body, head-body,
face of a draining honeycomb,
our four paper leaves, our pulp-dry,
still unopened hulls of sentences are
here and gone, our yellow hours are
gone. Your *shirtwaist*, my *school blouse*,
my one word for you, your middle fragrance,
apogee-effigy stalk.

WHAT IS THAT CRYING?

When I said I fell into the sea, sea said
one falls against one's shore. Everybody's water,
everything's flesh a little wind can lift.
A wave and a collar
have to curve. With succor,
as with a little forehead kiss,
two borders absorb. Unfasten the chain
behind your head. What is it not to see?
What was your mother's name?

ICE

Os, water's bone, instance of a thing held on,
as with the weight of words aplomb with carrying
their silent b's, things fecund
with self-crumbs: a womb's pomegranate secrecy
become the bulbous sounds a baby grows
from its place of every baby babbling, and
followed by the saying of a couple perfect words,
the voice glad-sounding, asking for a scissors or a tablet,
please. *Things may, may not hold on* was felt by everyone
taking positions in the field of the game
of childhood, cold there sometimes, enough
on the saddest nights to form inverted conifers at heart
around which a whole childhood firmed, became
hour-made, sharper, colder, older, strangely lighter,
from where some could barely stand a warmer touch,
would cry to hear a child say *don't cry*.

AUGUST

Should intention be the thread
each morning seems the one eye for, and should the thread
go slack, a longing to wait and see can overtake
the long-rehearsed longing to clarify, until
waiting for the next astonishment
returns again, almost enough,
a panting mockingbird held outside to
a bedroom window screen with its own feet,
gone through all its tracks, its open beak
turned toward another kind of radiance
the air conditioned room gives to the glass,
not hot. *It's hot everywhere but here*, is what
we think it thinks, the meshwork in its throat
another kind of screen, a scrim, another kind
of honeycomb. *You sing. I'm tired of singing. All songs*
are sweet. Time ruins everything.

THE DURATIONS

With the swinging lines of the crescent moon
upturned under the foot the Virgin shows
below her wooden, floor-length, sky-length robe,
and with the sound of fluttering inferred
by the travel of the crown-tailed fish
inside its kingdom in another, nearby room,
flickering an insoluble softness all these days
in a glass that carries always
the countenance of a sound that could be made
by something one could strike, could shatter,
with the memory of a music that entered us,
and the sinking in the silence afterward,
signal of the durations,
your silence and absence have form.

THIS WAY

No pre-
face;

face to
see through,

into which
shapes,

faces, odors,
colors, flavors

pass

under the day dome,

some tender.

things might have been otherwise. Everyone remembers
that time she walked in with flowers
sewn onto the hem of her dress, charming to all
but the flowers, and the fingers of outside light
now lacking those flowers to act upon, and the passerby bee
returning to find nothing there, and the drinking root
done drinking. Everyone knows *a backward step*
may not be taken into the realm of human hurt alone.
What she wore, moving from place to place,
seemed ordered by flowers whose kind she understood herself
not to be, but to be like, so palpably wished to be like
that she hoped she could be as fragrance is, sourced
in approach and dissipation, felt as form at heart.

SAY

Falling in a warm way
through all-day dusk not so unlike
the all-day sucker, flat, ribboned, coiled,
that she begged for as a child,
a rain continues
that waits for nothing, expects nothing,
deserves nothing.

SCHOOL

As though a group of persons looking at one bird
had called themselves a flock. For me, the wooden kitchen, made
right-sized, fragrant, smoothed, the shy wood knife
alive beside the wooden bowl of wooden fruits.
For me. So last night when the high curve
so long over my life curved down where I could see it briefly
in a dream, where into my old fear my mother again said
look out this pretty window I did see the backdrop whole
and almost finished rolling by: big wooden smiling sun,
wooden air nailed onto wooden hills, wooden birds inside the trees,
and then the edge, and then the single uncut tree, my afterlife.

THESE

She heard the dogs from her bed.
She closed the collar on her robe,
put on a hat she'd made,
dressed the old man
and brought him water. Bending at the waist,
he sang, weeping before and after.
I'm here drinking these tears, and today's secrets,
here with the secrets of dogs. The old man,
yes, is dressed. There is more water
and one old man. A hat made of sticks. And the dogs.

LION'S PAW

When I thought it wouldn't touch me,
I closed. All the close words of others were
as the air about me, the others unaware what it meant
to be indrawn, appearing indrawn as mere
reflex: gasp, yawn. Still, being come toward
sank into me and held me forward
like a latch made of thought
opening on a dreamed room dreamed before, or
closing on bars before fur,
hinged by my feeling of remembering the weight of a tail,
undulant, singular behind the legs. Say *lion's paw*
and a foreleg lifts in the general mind,
the fore always before the hind. In one life, how many
ever do come toward, and if mine is a seashell, light and dark,
orange-banded and rippling, wet or not, a bright handspan, love itself,
if it would not, if it will not touch me, some take their being from nothing,
and some say all things do.

THIS WAY

No pre-
face;

face that

alights,
alights on

twig-to-be-branch-

to-be-flute

(goes

softly around

bends)

farther

to follow

to follow

STUDY OF CIRRUS CLOUDS

after Constable's *Willy Lott's House, Near Flatford Mill*

It's too hard to say something only once. So says
John Constable's adamantine dog of paint,
of black paint thick on a brush made of fur
for the hind fur, white on another for the fore,
whose paws neither touch nor paint the ground,
though it seems otherwise. Light casts
doubt there. The same light emboldens
the house's front like a looker unwilling, finally,
to look away, brightening the house so wildly
the pond collapses in its shade. Know
I waited like a dog. I said my sayables over
like an olden door, like a dog, like a sky made
by clouds. I saw myself become a lace of spray.
Then a door opened on a friend, world-made,
sitting like a painting on the edge of my bed,
hair down, shirt off, who also let me really look,
who also could and did look back at me.

VELVET

The hours looked round when we checked them.
They felt round. They might have been tufts,
distinct and indifferent as breezes are,
but they rounded with simple walking
forward down the aisle
or back to the confessional where fragrance
like landscape comes, toward and away,
as from nerves inside folds of a body or a room
too easily drawn open by the movement of a drape,
plush as myrrh swung through the halo of a newborn
and eternal god, as though we could come back by having been,
swing our legs from our pew while our wedding is always going on,
not stay buried after every hooded, folded funeral, rounded by
the most private things in those hours we were entered while entering.

DAYS OF RAIN

His hand, moving in her, is the same hand
remembered by the other women, brought, oh,
closer than friends by it, who will not leave
the element of which they are a part,
dependent as ash on burning,
the mother first feeling him whole, drenched with herself,
born to say *out, go away from me* louder every year,
beside the girl who shone first, reeling, opening,
ash now, with the first wife radiant in her first eternity,
with every other always there, phosphorescences in sea water
once seen streaming in a wake, undulant, related, for the main,
apart from counting, saying *leave, but I will never leave.*

EMPIRICAL

From then on, thanks kept pouring in,
Odysseus lame and old.
Behind, to my waist, to my wrists,
still hang the thoughts I wove, as when
the clear-winged moth appeared in front of me,
a body fastened to nothing, neither contentment
nor contention as embellishment, threaded so
as to strike the mind of air and go,
or fold, so as to stay.

INVITATION TO TRAVEL

Did she get into bed again
or did she place the bed beneath herself,
could it be right to say
her hair spilled, are those rivulets the same
if she is a very young girl, if she is old
and in her dusk as a partner of order,
lilacs first then peonies
present though in another room,
are those rivulets
if, later, when listening with night,
the black dog's bark is heard as black
where she lies without need to be seen

THIS WAY

No pre-
face;

dream face
no one sees

(everyone

asleep). Eye, I
in-

side, held as
one was once

held: a-
bove a-

loft.

RED

Come back. Even as a shadow. Even as a dream. —Euripides, *Herakles*

Invariable gist of
red at the gate, then the gate all red.
Transferable, a
gamelan being played in the next room,
in the afterlife, round,
rounded, reciprocal.

SILVER MOORIT

Could the bare-faced sheep, a Merino, in moonlight,
say, with a moist mouth, *please, take my coat*,
the coat would fall to the shearsman at morning
the same. Could the spinning wheel sing the word *roving*
while swallowing it, we would pray with the nun
in her tub of warm milk, tray of fresh cookies just out of reach,
or remember the stray into woods as a child, bear in hand,
stuffed with wool, where a better child strayed
on a different day, far away from the others enough
to find odor of creosote private, like you,
on the footbridge still waiting forever, like me.
There could be more animal beauty to note, God to find,
bear in mind, a sense of things moving, the feeling
of cadence of feeling in thoughts, could be
two notes played together on the staff of a score,
a corral with a trough that encircles a fold.
To have made something, end. To be made something of,
some breeds have crimped fleeces so opulent, lustrous, so long,
they have almost no faces, but a view hid by locks
of a color of value called Silver Moorit.

EMERALD

Or the unlit green Epidote, miles from the mine,
deep under like sciatica, like the smell of Emeraude
in the confessional, Phthalo green going to black
inside the twilit creek, like the back room
at the Twombly, something under there
after the feeling of standing on fishes,
neither earthed nor unearthed, the third way
not yet formed or named.

GLOVE MY HAND

Locketed epoch, I am come to ask
after my grandmother's ringlets, released past her waist
in kelp-shapes by sea water, then drying
motionless but depicting flow, flowers of fish mouths
having earlier approached and opened about her legs
and closed. She was shored, perhaps,
thinking of Freud's head opened at the mouth
by song, or of all water grained to mist
floating in an effort to drop back down, with so much
sorted by forces and duration, maybe shaken as I was
on a perfect day, hidden behind the furnace reading Salinger,
able to be wiped out of the book of the living.

THEORY OF A NEST

Theory of a nest made to hold a nest
hand-woven of palm in the shape of a gourd
with an entrance to which no bird will come,
                                                                        of a fossil
called deer heart, human heart-sized, passed from friend's hand
to friend's hand, up from the ground and still ground,
up from water, past water, the umbo facing itself in a nod
as one fiddlehead would say to another *yes, we are the shape*
we make,
            of cloth opening for a button made from shell, fastening
or un-, another semi-permanence easily undone,
                                                                              of a bodice flower
woven in, or worn as scent alone, or picked, pinned, all
gone by day or night, days and nights
the name that lasts longest comes to be.

HOLDING WHITE

Veil in the eyes of the nearly-gone,
iris/clitoris at its wall, all
the peonies up but unopened at the graves, and
someone's someone remembering
to serve the table
Soursop flower, Butterprint,
Horse Tongue, Christ's Thorn,
Convolvulus, Summer's Bride.

SHE SAW

Between a bird and a leaf sits death. —Yannis Ritsos

She saw with one eye marked for lamentation,
white flower centered by a core of blue
with gray that rose according to,
like the brindled charms one hopes on, verdure
in order, a flux of barriers within a bush of barriers,
like a house one rents and hopes to weight
with an agile temperament by the arrangement
of low chairs. But always, beyond that,
her other eye was marked for flight
as the curve from thing to thing requires.

IF WE MAY

Let us remain for a moment
on this border so gently touching
this other one. The children are speaking
forever to the parents who hear and say
the same in return: It's good you are
where you are. Fewer presents
of glass along the iron road
makes sense. All the old languages
are sober now. You look, like a dog
in a suit, at once old and young
for your age.

THIS WAY

No pre-
face;

face that

looked at

all I
saw,

seeing as
me.

Looked back

at or
not,

I was

made / more.

EPITHALAMIUM

At the boundary of
the cornfield the windbreak stands.
The corn is in order, aligned,
processional. The windbreak
is wilder but also planned,
holds at heart a bank
of feral roses, white, tangled,
voluptuous, liturgical, with flower heads
like mouths open or opening
past words, ecstatic,
immortal as the fragrance
of a rose. How fine they are,
but not as beautiful
as those two animals I saw one day
eating them to live.

SIT

From a chair, a shoe
is seen under the bed
a boy dreamed through
his childhood and left.
It is her shoe, she
who brought good nights
who sees, who leaves it there.

ELSE

Who in the house, as always
without sentences?
Who cried her eyes out, missing her mom?
Who tapped the wrist where the bracelet
had been worn? Who pointed
to the drawing of the man? Who waved,
meaning *say hello to your new girlfriend*
who drew that, who made my bracelet
that I put away.

PERENNIAL

Erotic quick-slow of flowers wave
just past the garden chair.
Ganglia and tendrils swell
at the margins of my person
and my lawn. In a flowered dress
let me account for dying before
you could find me; like light from the moon
I would sit, golden and almost close
before I changed to gray. My garden
never was me; it was feral with flowers
and in every light, aroused. Who's left
struggles with what could be meaningful next;
little petals want nothing. Little petals
are laces of colors and laces of scents
that come back to unlace all that holds them.

AFTER OR BECAUSE

After or because she embellished
the green linen arms, a green close to
the green of the puppet's wood face so
well held between wings of black hair,
after she sewed down by hand
smallest glass beads at the points
where she'd crossed the gold threads on the arms
as she liked, a net fixed to the forearms as sleeves,
because she fitted the puppet's hands with further puppets,
barn swallows of cloth, one for each, navy velvet above,
cream and rust underneath, tender in paleness underneath,
she was met with a barn swallow briefly on a rail
not awaiting the resurrection of the dead.

THIS WAY

No pre-
face. One

face to
lift to

someone's
head's way

(heads sway).
Lifted,

lowered:
two ways

pain got
in. O

dreamy forces
of the ever

still essences,
be with us.

RETURN

So little, so lithe, a skirt lifted
by twirling, that's how you returned
in my sleep beyond your death. Pink wall
that has to have a door that locks.
Odor of lilacs warm and doubled in a vase.
If only we hadn't killed someone,
but who, and did we divide the money
equally? We did not. We recounted it,
out loud as the little kids
and clocks that charm the hours do.

THIS WAY

No pre-
face;

tincture of

unguent of

making

light spool
onto

the next

mortal

thing.

LIGHT PINK OCTAGON

(Richard Tuttle, 1967)

We looked, we looked away
to private lives, for after-images
of what our look had poised
among our thoughts, not a rose
opening among thoughts of roses opening
nor the seizure of rose-scent in an arid place;
it was more clear than the collective recollection,
and cleaner than we are, and it leaned
as a kite seems to, toward and away. Now to
remember the impossible: entirety of girlishness,
grief made mellifluous, kitemother here *and* gone.

THE AERIALIST

It was the shoulders. Every
feather hurt. My souvenir?
Joy, swung out over the blades,
swings back, though in time it goes out
a little less far, joy demurred of itself
like down, or amazement felt receding
far below. It was always night for me,
me twinkling like the star we all
learned rhyme upon, love coming
to itself but as a different self,
like flying but not flying,
expensive, too far, though I was
sure I was a diamond in the sky.

IN

Although she had avoided being alone with him,
that very fact made him feel that he was still alive within her.
—Yasunari Kawabata (*Beauty and Sadness*)

It was as though the day took heart again, as from having to look inward
in order to go out, and in exchange for having made,
the day before, a chaparral bird step easily overhead, across the gaps
between the cedar branches set as open ceiling on the porch.
The bird was fabulous, wood-colored against the wood, sure-
footed, long-narrowed at the tail, sharp at the head, which turned,
and there came the yellow ring around the eye and sustenance,
a nestling caught and dangling from the mouth. Take
heart. The day, like every day, was flourishing. There was
a painted Magdalene with an egg in hand, a red egg to be understood
to be the egg of resurrection, she, most loved, was first to see by holding fast
to a closed door. But did the bird who made the egg have thoughts? Holy Spirit,
keep speaking in birdsong. A different painting makes her hold a jar of unguent up,
her under-hand assigned to tenderness and confidence; the over,
on the lid, lifting to a crack, is made grotesque by what she knows.
In exchange for something unidentified, in the Book of Mary,
Mary wrote *I saw the Lord in a vision and I said to Him, Lord*
I saw you today in a vision. This way the nestling dies and lives.

POOR BOY LONG WAYS FROM HOME

As though understanding the space music can transport us to,
the woods grew dark. Had the birds,
minus flying, minus song, asked to stop being birds? The trail
gave way. The hint of wild onions soft-speared through,
crows became branches and a fox
looked around, and a hidden bear picked up the scent
of cream horns being eaten in a car two states away
while I turned on the path to go home
and was afraid, though passing under normal trees as always,
but afraid I'd come too far. From up ahead, someone I loved
came walking toward, but awkwardly, holding and being held by
someone I didn't know. Hello. The crow
shook out its leaves. I was only sorry
I had forgotten to seem glad for them, who passed
as tendrils intertwined but cut away, by the creek of tears where
the wild onions touch each spring as they had and would again.

IMPARTIAL THEME

All day, the long-armed kite makers come toward.
Their thoughts have rustled high above tall domes,

and low below the curve. One wonders
what an eave is for. Evening arrives,

the wind dies lower, lower down.
Your tired arms in reposition, in repose,

let holding go. Let go; turn off the lamp
in baritone, and sigh the mind's fire out.

The window's up. Your sleep is in your room with you. Night
night. Now can the wild deer arrive, one-two, at windowside

on grass dried thicker, later than last year's. So long,
they stand behind the sounds their word-like chewing makes,

two words repeated, floated into you,
joined, estranged, the crossbar of a life
not yet arrived or understood.

FOR

She pointed; *ask*. But who goes close to the river
while rain meets itself there as other water?
How would I go, like a rumor? Heard, or unsaid?
Is a bone whistle not still a bone?
Can a window, like a mirror, not reflect?
Not in place of me, nor as me, nor on my behalf. Not
through me. In front of me, ask. Ask for me.

ANISE FROM VENUS

Only after offering his name
could Odoardo Beccari write this down: *a black dye*
can be made from the large juicy leaves
of a Medinillopsis Beccariana. Like him,
the night sky engendered of itself a special meteor
and let it fall. It was less electrical
than lightning, much more sweet, without applause

except that it was also seen
reflected on the stilled face of a lake,
and so had happened twice at once, a riddle maybe
lovers understand. The dead
may have had to look away.

In a Nahua voice, a story goes:
a man evades the Lightnings
(who take a shortcut to catch him)
by putting on the best cape, finest cape,
because the Lightnings wear only the ordinary ones,

the same way a painter sees, or catches stories of,
or dreams a certain meteor and paints, anonymous,
one night sky as the lushest, closest cloak
a lake and a redoubled heart can understand

while the flowering anise, never singular, at night
exudes itself in star-fields, out of hand,
inside, under, outside itself, very gently
skyward, earthward, licorice and pale,
more joyous than the asphodel.
Where audible, a choir of the soft cries cries.

Lake eyes, fragrant mouths.
Beccari said a black dye can be made
from the juicy leaves that touched his name
seeing the Dayak at the heart of Borneo
use the juice of these to blacken out their teeth,

another and another wreath of exhalations bending in
night sky, dark lake, fine cape, drenched kiss
of the afterlife of memory
and the mirror found again.

DOMINUS

A dusty house. A mohair
or angora. Easy to feel
the smallest things as more or less
a network of networks, a dominion
leading to a domination of things
or thoughts on things, should the cat
come out and sit in a sunbeam
with a sky of dust motes alive
above her head, all the dreams dreamed
in one life until now, so small
that only one can see them, each
a falling shimmer and a domino.

FOLLOW BACK

The table in the woods
is made of wood. Not for nothing,
the night violets dust the ground
at the lower limit of the heights night makes
as trees make, in darkness, themselves more
liquid at heart. Who would, waving over,
burrow vibration into everything below
better than these cicadas do? Your dead,
my dead fan in and sit with us. Don't laugh.
Don't leave. Time has unfolded all of us.
Who but you would say this is the secret place I think
I'll fold myself to pleats inside of you.

DATE OF BIRTH

Where have you been, what did you do
to make yourself appear? Summer's moment
was over; the way was made for larger weather
by the day you were born. Without self-sacrifice
you appeared; no one in the room
was smaller or less ephemeral. Marble of earth
who grew to be the astronaut who said
the earth is like a marble. Perfume of forests
way down there. Temples to the right
and left of the eyes like everyone. Rose, ruby,
cheek, lip. You kept pressing, being told
the sun doesn't lower itself down.
You recognized death straightaway as
guaranteed by every miracle. You, embryo.
You, kite-mother's daughter. You, hushed baby
sailor in calm weather, seeking out the one
who will offer another bag of wind.

NOTES

"Roses Are Planted Where Thorns Grow" takes its title from William Blake's *The Marriage of Heaven and Hell.* Lines 16 and 17 quote from Robert Duncan's poem "Tears of St. Francis."

"Play of Causes" takes its title from the poem "Dawn" by Jean Follain, translated by W. S. Merwin.

Lines 9–16 in "Two Horses in a Field with Daffodils" borrow from *Scienza Nuova* by Giambattista Vico, written in 1744, as translated from the third edition by Thomas Goddard Bergin and Max Harold Fisch, Ithaca, 1970, titled *The New Science of Giambattista Vico,* and referenced in E. H. Gombrich's *The Preference for the Primitive: Episodes in the History of Western Taste and Art* (London and New York: Phaidon, 2002), p. 59.

"Mobile" is for Carter Smith.

"I Don't Know How to Make a Man" takes its title from Roberto Juarroz' *First Vertical Poetry,* section 13, translated by W. S. Merwin. Line 7 is from Yasumari Kawabata's story, "Oil," translated by J. Martin Holman. The italicized sentence in lines 10 and 11 was found in *The Book of Symbols,* published by Taschen. The last line is Emerson's, from *Man the Reformer.*

"At Intervals" is for Corinne Lee.

"For All She Knew" contains a quote (lines 7 and 8) from Elaine Scarry's *The Body in Pain* (Oxford University Press, 1985), p. 148.

"These" is after Yannis Ritsos' poem "Laugh."

In "Study of Cirrus Clouds," the phrase "lace of spray" is from Gaston Bachelard's essay "The Dynamics of Landscape": "Poetic legend is fond of repeating how Aphrodite was born from the foaming waves; whiteness and a lace of spray suffice for the poet to make a woman . . ."

"Light Pink Octagon" was written for The Blanton Museum of Art in Austin, Texas, where it is exhibited beside Richard Tuttle's sculpture of the same name.

"Poor Boy Long Ways from Home" is also the title of a traditional blues song of unknown origin.

The italics in the last two lines of "For" relate to Jacques Derrida's *Sovereignties in Question: The Poetics of Paul Celan* (New York: Fordham University Press, 2005).

The set of poems titled "This Way" corresponds to a series of "Powder Books," each also constructed in a powder compact as a token of thanks to others whose words have guided mine. Short videos of the "Powder Books" can be seen here: www.kathleenpeirce.com.

"This Way" (p. 9) is for Leigh Shelton.
"This Way" (p. 23) is for Catherine Barnett.
"This Way" (p. 29) is for Jean Valentine.
"This Way" (p. 35) is for Mary Gordon.
"This Way" (p. 41) is for Alison Cimino.
"This Way" (p. 47) is for Fanny Howe.
"This Way" (p. 56) is for Jorie Graham.
"This Way" (p. 62) is for Saskia Hamilton.
"This Way" (p. 64) is for Courtney Simchak.